Hooves Touch the Wind

Hooves Touch the Wind

Riding Above the Dirt in Life

Grace Atherton

Bestwine
Press

A BESTWINE PRESS BOOK
© 2025 Grace Atherton

Scripture texts are taken from the New King James Version® (NKJV). Copyright © 1982 by Thomas Nelson. Used by permission. All rights reserved.

Scriptures in artwork on page 55 taken from King James Version (KJV), public domain.

Front and back top cover photos: Max & Maxwell Equestrian Photography
Horse (*Pickles*): Equestrian Adventures of Florida
Nails: Emerald Spa & Nails
Dress (*Poetry*): Don't Stress The Dress
Author photo: Mark Watson/Spotlight Photography

ISBN: 979-8-9921838-1-8

Contents

Introduction

Acknowledgments

1. Hitting Dirt: Unfelt Value...1

2. A Mess Up: Sprout Power..7

3. Eat It: Think to Be..13

4. Picture-Perfect Dream: Imagine It..............................19

5. Pain in a Parking Lot: Reframe to Gain......................25

6. Joy on the Journey: Laughter Heals............................31

7. Unlikely Friends: Free to Fly.......................................35

8. Buried Alive: People Along the Way............................41

9. Gratitude: What Matters...49

10. My Ride or Die: Search for the Answer.......................53

11. Died for Dirt: Love's Everything.................................61

12. Scars to Stars: Imprinted for Purpose.......................67

13. Bulletproof Dream: Stars Shine.................................75

Riding Lessons..81

About Grace Atherton: I Know What It's Like.................83

References...86

Introduction

I never planned to write this book.

Sometimes when you are living life, it can be hard to sit back and think, *Wow, this will be impactful to anyone.*

I actually started out talking about and writing small parts of my story on social media. Surprisingly, the keys I shared helped others overcome their own struggles.

It got to the point where I had people privately contacting me around the clock for advice.

Finally, I realized I had to think of a more efficient way to reach all those requesting help to rise above their challenges.

One recurring request that came over and over was to write a book and include what helped me through my challenges.

At first, I declined.

Writing a book can be a huge task, but that was not what made it so daunting.

I knew if I wrote my story, I would have to relive some moments I didn't want to face.

Besides, I kind of got used to the privacy I enjoyed when I talked one-on-one, apart from social media, where I could customize the parts of my story I shared that would be most helpful.

Finally, by writing, I didn't want anyone to think that I am beyond learning and try to put me on a pedestal in a position I could never live up to.

So, I continued to say no. Until I could say no, no more!

In the following, you will get to know more of my journey than I have shared publicly.

Before I get too far, however, I would like to clarify that I am not a therapist, doctor, counselor, or psychiatrist (although I have learned from many of these individuals and believe they all have their place when needed).

In this book, I share personal development advice that has helped me and others overcome life's challenges. Your own personal research, discretion, and best judgment are always advised, as each person is unique and requires individual solutions.

I hope the lessons in the following pages begin to propel you to rise above the dirt in your past to reach your unique destination on your ride of life. You, the horse, and I all have something in common: We were born to fly!

- Grace Atherton

Acknowledgments

Special thanks to the following:

My parents for reading and editing my papers as I grew up, giving me a desire to learn and helping me be a better writer.

Joseph and Bethany for truly seeing who I am and encouraging my individuality. Bethany, also thank you for co-authoring Chapter 7 with me.

Rita Richmond for your support whenever I wanted to quit, for always encouraging the best in me, and for taking the pictures in Chapter 2.

Ally for typing and editing my writing and for being there during the hardest time of my life. I'm proud of you for going after your dream of being a nurse so others can benefit from your gift.

Eli for helping me write the vision for this book in January 2022 and for helping me learn some lessons during that time in my life.

Antoinette for always believing in me and being a huge part of my journey.

Elonzio and Nicole for letting me share your Mom, Antoinette's story and how we crossed paths.

Kelly for editing the book, for all your support and encouragement, and for believing in this project from the start.

Wendy, LoraLee, Chinaza, Judy, and Shelia for your support and encouragement on this project and through the years. Shelia, as I write this, I still have the old-fashioned quill pen you gave me on my desk to remind me I am a writer.

For **countless mentors** around the world who have taught me so much in life.

Rashaan and Anthony for being my accountability colleagues and family in business and for all the meetings.

Mary Jo Gremling of Bestwine Press for helping me fine tune my book outline and encouraging me to use my authentic voice, creativity, and style.

Jennifer Toegel of Max & Maxwell Equestrian Photography (a subdivision of Jennifer Juniper Photography LLC) for taking the cover images.

Jennifer Miko of Equestrian Adventures of Florida and Team for providing the horse, **Pickles**, from your famous beach rides to be featured on the cover.

Emerald Spa & Nails (Ormond Beach, Florida) for collaborating to do my nails for the photo shoot.

Don't Stress the Dress for renting out the dress (called "Poetry") used on the cover.

Rob Chiola Films and Team for doing the horse videography when the cover pictures were taken.

Mark Watson of Spotlight Photography for taking the author photo.

And countless other friends and family! I appreciate you all more than you know!

I dedicate this book ...

To my Grandmother Scott—Your love, creativity, humor, authenticity, and encouragement live on with me even though you've left this world. I hope this book helps future generations as well. I miss you!

To You—the down and out. The one covered in the dirt of life. The one who knows there's more to life but feels trapped in your past. The one who has experienced more trauma and pain in your life than you can measure.

This book is dedicated and written specifically for you. This is what I would have told myself back then and what I wish I could have learned sooner. I have walked in your boots, and my hope is that through the following pages you will gain at least one insight that helps you ride above the dirt in your past.

Hitting Dirt: Unfelt Value

It's amazing how a day can change the course of your life.

June 28, 2015, was that day for me.

Inside a store, I stared at the gun case. I didn't care what I bought, just something small enough to do the job.

On the way there, as I drove in my car alone in the pouring rain, I cried out loud, "If there is still a plan and purpose for my life, stop me—because I can't stop myself!"

It's hard to explain, but I was powerless to stop the racing, intrusive thoughts. This was it. Hopelessness and depression were coursing through every vein of my body until I felt suicide was the ONLY way out.

For weeks leading up to this night, I sat on my bed alone in a house and later in an apartment. I could feel evil all around me, and dark thoughts completely enveloped my mind. I researched ways to end my life, fell into an addiction, and thought of how I could change my identity to be unrecognizable.

I even considered shaving my head, which was opposite to my typical personality since I've always loved long hair.

I wanted to take my life so I could get rid of the pain inside. At the time, I didn't feel I could do even one thing right. All I could feel was rejection and unforgiveness toward myself.

My relationships were gone. My health was gone. My dream job was gone. My innocence was gone. My desire to do or be anything was gone. My dreams were gone. Everything was going wrong.

> **I wanted to take my life so I could get rid of the pain inside.**

My sleep was sporadic and interrupted by nightmares, anxiety, flashbacks, and panic attacks that made it hard to breathe. I cried all the time and could hardly eat. I just wanted to forget, disappear, and not exist anymore.

Slowly, I started to pull away and not talk to anyone as much as possible outside of work. A relative tried to push in to get me to the doctor, who mentioned the possibility of a brain tumor. One night, while the same relative was driving me somewhere, I yelled at her to let me out of the car so I could end it. I was done.

And so, in the end, in that store, I found myself staring face to face at a gun. This was it.

Suddenly, out of nowhere, my thoughts were interrupted. From behind me and the glass gun case, a voice spoke. "You don't look like the gun type of girl."

Wearing boots, jeans, and a shirt, I thought, *You have to be kidding me. If I don't look like it right now, nobody does.*

Finally, the second time the voice spoke, I turned around and stepped back. The guy at the store was quietly saying, "No" and pointing at me. Slowly, I backed away and left.

As the windshield wipers scraped across my car's glass, clearing away the torrential rain, I couldn't help but realize that something had carried me through this storm when I couldn't carry myself.

A few nights later, I "randomly" came across an inspirational video online. From there, I started on my learning journey to invest in the most valuable asset I never knew I had: myself. I researched and learned. Over time I began to find real answers that helped me find hope and get out of the darkest time in my life.

Maybe you can relate to that story in some way. Maybe it describes you in some area. Or maybe you have been there in the not-so-recent past or at some time in your life. Where you felt everything was falling apart but you didn't know what to do. Where you felt hopeless. Perhaps that moment is today where you know you need something more. Something to get you unstuck from the dirt in life so you can make it. I understand, because that's where I was— desperate for change. I knew if I didn't find that change, I was done.

If this is you, I want you to know I don't believe in accidents. I don't believe you came across this book randomly, just as I don't believe I found resources years ago, some of which were books. Although every story is different with various searches for answers, I believe some of the lessons I uncovered during my time of "hitting dirt" will be helpful for you too in your unique journey.

My hope is that through sharing my experiences and the "riding lessons" that helped me overcome, I can help you begin to make it above the dirt in your life too.

I believe, just like me, you can go from the dust in your life to the clouds. I believe you can rise instead of hiding in despair or shame. I believe you can feel alive again in life—thrive, not just survive.

You, the horse, and I all have something in common. We were born to fly!

Riding Lesson #1

Commit to investing time in yourself, especially to learn. You are priceless, whether you feel like it or not!

Do You Hear the Whisper

Don't give up,
Just take it one day at a time,
Do the next thing,
Look at what you have left.

Do you hear the whisper ...

Others have made it,
You will do the same,
You are made for a purpose,
It won't end today in the grave.

Do you hear the whisper ...

The storm can't stop you,
The darkness can't hide you,
The lightning won't end you,
The tears of rain won't last forever.

Do you hear the whisper ...

The abuse doesn't define you,
The shame can't forever find you,
Don't drown yourself in other things—
Even if you're living in uncertainty.

Do you hear the whisper ...

You still have gifts to give the world,
You still have breath,
Your heart is still beating,
You are worth more than silver or gold.

Do you hear the whisper...

There is help just ahead,
The dark clouds will be breaking,
Light will be coming,

And the sun will be shining instead.

A Mess Up: Sprout Power

*"For there is hope for a tree, if it is cut down,
that it will sprout again, and that its tender shoots
will not cease." – Job*

I could never have planned that day. It was July 11, 2023.

As I was doing my morning routine, the above quote randomly came to mind. I thought about how no matter what comes in life, there is a possibility of a comeback, just like a tree cut down can regrow and live again.

It was just a passing thought as I continued through that day. Imagine my surprise when later, as I looked out my window, I saw it.

It was around twenty years old. Some had tried to burn it, leaving a layer of charcoal around the top. Others had tried to dig it up. Around the edges and in the middle were gashes where some had tried to chop it into pieces. It was the epitome of gone. Twenty long years. A mere dead, dried out, unwanted stump.

I pulled up the window shades to look more closely. To my surprise, in the middle of the stump stood something: a new little evergreen tree. It was wild, because there were no similar trees around it from which it could have been seeded.

I immediately recalled the words I had thought about earlier in the day: the wisdom of Job, the man of ancient times who lost everything—family, health, house, and money—and then got back double.

As I continued to stare at the tree, I saw it as an example of hope and overcoming impossibility. Looking back, I can definitely see that, just like the tree, we have such a thing as sprout power. An ability to come back even on the ruins of what happened and the ability to regrow stronger in the very areas of past defeat.

To me, the stump represents the times in life where everything goes down in ashes. Everything that was built, grown, and struggled for. It represents the years gone by that seemingly smashed any hope of something good coming out of the bad. It represents the experiences, words, and thoughts that made it feel impossible to dream of something better than the mess. On top of that, it represents the mess made by outward conditions—the digging, burning, chopping in life that leave a low expectation of the future.

The most amazing thing is how potential inside of us—despite the losses, the gashing situations, the fire, the words that cut us down, and the digging that tried to root us out—is still there.

What was placed inside the tree—and inside each person before they had a body and hit planet Earth, regardless of time and circumstances—can still grow again.

In the stump and the loss is life. Life that can sprout and go up again, creating beauty from ashes.

With water and sun (the right environment, nutrients, and input), it can overcome every obstacle and become more. More than a stump. More than its past, which is now its fuel. More than its experiences. More than the words. More than the failures. More than the mess. More than the things that died and went down. In the stump and the loss is life. Life that can sprout and go up again, creating beauty from ashes.

I hope the picture of a tree sprouting from a stump helps you too. I hope it helps you realize that in the very places you have been knocked down are the very areas you have the potential to grow and be even stronger. The further you fell, the higher you can grow. Your hopes, dreams, and potential, though invisibly buried inside—perhaps so deep you can't see them anymore—outwardly chopped on and burned, can still come back.

You are more. More than your memories. More than the negative words. More than your mistakes. More than what knocked you down. More than a stump. Inside of you is potential. You were made with "sprout power," the ability to get back up and grow stronger right on the ugly mess. You are made for more.

"For there is hope for a tree,
If it is cut down, that it will sprout again,
And that its tender shoots will not cease.
Though its root may grow old in the earth,
And its stump may die in the ground,
Yet at the scent of water it will bud
And bring forth branches like a plant."

- Job
(a man who lost everything and got back double)

Riding Lesson #2

Purpose is inside you. Do not wait for the perfect time or conditions. Grow and bloom on and in the mess.

Preparation: The Pain Is for a Purpose

It was placed on the inside before it hit planet Earth,
Each layer, each pattern, each vibrant piece.

It wasn't accidental the dark and the loneliness,
Where everything was covered up and unseen.

It hurt to push through and often it wondered would it make it,
Would it have enough breath or would it die here?

Although some relief made its way down,
It took so much time to get to the surface and the light.

Even up higher it still felt useless at times,
A mere shadow of a figure in the entire existence.

Time passed and more time until,
Expanded in so many directions, it covered the horizon.

Finally each piece pushed its way open and lo and behold,
All the pain was for a reason
because in full scale who could deny the purpose.

The weirdest truth of all though is ...
In the seed all along was everything in time to produce the rose!

Inside is everything you need for your destiny ...
The pain, darkness, and mess are for a purpose.
Nothing is wasted!

Eat It: Think to Be

It's easy to see the outward actions and patterns in our own or others' lives. Although we all have things we want or need to change, sometimes it's hard to pinpoint how to change or what's causing the repeated pattern or cycle.

That was me years ago in one area: food. At that time, I had a picture in my mind of what I considered the "perfect body." That image was unrealistically thinner and taller than my natural build.

As a result, I started starving myself and eating as little as possible to try to reach that goal. When I did eat because I was hungry, I would try to force myself to throw up afterward. Besides that, I exercised constantly, running up to ten miles a day. As you can imagine, I was exhausted and sick much of the time.

No matter how much weight I lost, when I looked in the mirror, I was not thin enough for the unrealistic picture that had taken over my mind. I was obsessed with food because I was constantly hungry and trying not to eat.

Eventually, my body flipped (because my metabolism was messed up) and started holding onto all the food I ate, causing me to gain and retain extra weight. Without the right nutrients, including healthy fats, being anorexic caused me to spiral into depression, question my body image, and have suicidal thoughts for the first time in my life. (Thankfully, I no longer deal with those issues.)

This pattern seemed to go on for years, even though I was trying every weight loss program and brainstorming everything I knew to figure out a solution and reach my goal.

One day I sat at an event. I wasn't paying much attention until the speaker brought out an easel and drew some huge brown marks through the picture he had painted, seemingly messing it up. I scooted to the edge of my seat to watch. From my perspective, he had ruined his painting and made it ugly. He mentioned something to the effect of that's how some of us view our lives. I could definitely relate.

> *Being a perfectionist, that is how I saw myself. ... If my life was a painting, I felt it was definitely messed up.*

Being a perfectionist, that is how I saw myself. Besides dealing with anorexia, I dealt with crooked overlapping teeth (not getting braces until after high school). If my life was a painting, I felt it was definitely messed up.

So I listened to the speaker. At the conclusion of his talk, he spoke about how the ugly marks he'd added to the painting represented being grateful for and accepting who we are currently, whether anything ever changed in life or not. But he also said we should realize that no matter what we saw, our life's painting wasn't done yet. Then he proceeded to transform the ugly marks and "mistakes" into beautiful trees, water, and flowers, making his picture even more beautiful.

That day, he gave us a challenge I'll never forget. With tears streaming down my face and fear in my heart, I decided to do the challenge. It was a change in my mindset. It was accepting who I was currently. That day, I decided that even if nothing ever changed, I would eat, regardless of the physical outcome on my body.

That day nothing outwardly changed, but inwardly I felt light as a feather as the mental weight of carrying a burden over food lifted.

Whenever thoughts came up about my body afterward, I decided I would say, "I am perfectly made."

Within months, I lost weight while I was doing minimal exercise and eating three balanced meals a day. In fact, I wasn't even focused on food, exercise, or weight anymore. Its importance had left my life, and I was happy inwardly without looking to my outward appearance to determine that joy.

I decided I would say, "I am perfectly made."

Today I've been asked to do classy modeling for several photographers and picked to join an agency through acting, modeling, and singing (though I declined the latter). I'm still blown away when someone tells me I am beautiful, because I haven't always looked this way.

Thankfully, none of our paintings are done yet even today in every area of our life, but we can accept where we are regardless of mistakes or what we consider imperfections and know that our life's story is not finished yet. Then our life can turn into something surprisingly beautiful, just like the artwork I saw transformed that day.

Riding Lesson #3

Accept yourself fully without comparison. Then work on the thoughts, emotions, and words you are feeding your mind and mouth about yourself and your life.

A New Start

Seeds are what make oaks,
Words are what make speeches,
Letters are what make books,
Drops are what make oceans.

Strokes are what make paintings,
Movements are what make Olympians,
Notes are what make songs,
Ingredients are what make dishes.

Everything starts in minimal form,
The smallest possible beginning,
It's the start that seems the least important,
But added to time it compounds into bigger pieces.

The words we speak, good or bad,
Come back in maximum form.
It's said you can count the seeds in an apple,
But you can't count the apple trees in the seed.

In other words, the actions we put out into the world,
Will come back to us later in multiplication,
Creating results, branches and leaves,
And more fruit and seeds that will go out again.

It's the small tears cried in times of pain
That bring about harvest of joy in sheaves of grain,
Watching content changes hearts and minds,
What we allow out of our mouths transforms our physical lives.

The ripple effect of each action, thought, emotion, and word
Is felt throughout time, ages, and places.
May we think about everything we do,
Because it's the seed of a start that changes spaces.

Picture-Perfect Dream: Imagine It

There are some pictures that make you smile and cry in a good way. The pictures on the cover of this book do that for me.

To me these pictures represent more than a moment caught in time.

They represent something I dreamed about while I went through physical rehabilitation on and off for two years after I experienced two car wrecks between June 2022 and June 2023.

Before taking the cover photos, I had two pictures that kept my hope alive for complete recovery in spite of negative reports.

One of the pictures was of a woman in a white dress on a white horse on the beach, close to what I imagined in my mind.

The other picture was of a princess warrior from a movie.

I would look at those pictures and imagine physically getting back and riding a horse on the beach, though I had never actually ridden on a beach. When negative thoughts or pain would come, especially after another physical therapy session—and even more intensely after negative reports when I had to start from ground zero again after a second wreck—I would look at those images and tell myself that was me and I would ride again.

Fast forward to when my dream finally became a reality. I had a sponsored trip to Florida. Before going, I contacted photographers on the internet. One stood out. Her name was Jennifer Toegel. She's a world-class wedding photographer who is also going after her dream of horse photography with her company, Max & Maxwell Equestrian Photography (a subdivision of Jennifer Juniper Photography LLC).

> *I would look at those images and tell myself that was me and I would ride again.*

She immediately agreed to take the cover photos for this book.

I showed Jennifer the two pictures I had looked at constantly that gave me so much hope through physical rehab, and she brought them to life.

As the sun set on the beach in Florida, I'll never forget mounting bareback a beautiful white horse named Pickles. He is one of the horses Jennifer Miko uses for her famous beach rides with her dream company, Equestrian Adventures of Florida. We took the front cover picture and then saddled Pickles up for a fast ride across the beach.

The scene from the saddle was breathtaking. I felt a mixture of excitement and freedom. It was a dream come true!

Today, no matter what you are facing, consider this: Who would you be and what would you do if anything was possible?

Over the years, I have recorded dreams in different ways. Sometimes it has been listing goals by categories. Here are some I've used: *Spiritual, Personal Development, Character, Health, Fitness, Fun, Financial, Contribution, Creativity,* and *Friendships.* I have also drawn simple pictures or found images as I did when I dreamed of riding a horse on a beach. In addition, I have found recordings of movie scenes or songs that inspired me.

The main thing is you want to not only stick to dreams that seem possible but put down things that are impossible and start using your imagination again. Over and over, I have seen these dreams come true in my life and others' lives as creative opportunities have opened up. Sometimes it takes time, and you may want to change some dreams in the process, but there's nothing like sitting down and writing down a list of dreams. They create hope for a better tomorrow.

Today, if you haven't already, take time to list a few goals or maybe even get a picture to help you visualize your picture-perfect dream to get back into the saddle of your life.

Riding Lesson #4

Dream again. Write, draw, picture, or record what you would do if you had all the money, time, and energy in the world.

When Did Your Dream Stop?

When did your dream stop?
When did you think it could never happen,
When did you believe your life was not worth another day,
When did your unique talents get pushed out of the way?

When did your dream stop?
The imagination of your childhood or adulthood,
The things, though they were out there,
Did not seem impossible or even too heavy to bear?

When did your dream stop?
Was it the words or actions by someone close or a leader over you,
Was it the painful experiences, trauma, or abuse?
When did you think trying was no longer of any use?

When did your dream stop?
Was it a moment,
Was it slowly day by day,
Or was it sudden when you had nothing left to say?

When did your dream stop?
Was it when you reached the pinnacle,
Of all that you had planned,
And suddenly you didn't realize you could start again?

When did your dream stop?
Was it the diagnosis or the accident,
The shuffling of the plans,
Or the addiction that left a dent?

When did your dream stop?
Was it a failure or mistake,
The inability to forgive yourself,
Or thinking you didn't have what it takes?

When did your dream stop?
Was it the loss of a loved one,
The bills piling up a case,
Or that one door, closed in your face?

When did your dream stop?
How about never,
Not today, not tomorrow
Not ever!

Pain in a Parking Lot: Reframe to Gain

I didn't think I was going to be emotional, until I drove by the parking lot and my mind wandered back to a moment.

That moment was January 4, 2002. I was fourteen years old.

That day, some of my younger siblings and I stayed in a van as my mom went grocery shopping. The van was parked near the front of the parking lot, a seemingly safe place in our small town.

We were just laughing and listening to music when suddenly we saw a man. He was dressed in khaki pants and a blue collared shirt and exited a truck near us. I didn't pay much attention until he walked around our entire vehicle and peered in the dark, tinted windows. Getting to the passenger side, he demanded that we open the door.

As I stared into his eyes, I could see and feel the darkness controlling him that glared back at me. It shook me to my core.

One sibling unlocked the door. Quickly, I hit the button on the door, hoping it would relock. It did. I prayed under my breath as I muttered the word, "No." After a long standoff of words, where he used every excuse possible to get in (including that we hit his vehicle), he walked to the store front. It was not over yet though.

Sitting on a bench with his hands crossed, he angrily stared at us. Finally, after what felt like an eternity, he disappeared into the store. I immediately wanted to get help, but I was afraid he would reappear.

At that point, another man came out and began to put his groceries in his car trunk. Quickly, I told the new man what had happened and asked him to watch. Nonchalantly, he did. I went into the store and found my Mom, and we reported the incident to a manager who also seemed unconcerned about it.

Years later, I drove by the same store where the attempted abduction had happened when I was a kid. I saw the parking lot and reminisced. I also thought about other moments in other places where I had faced similar evil later on in life. I hadn't planned to be in that city, but here I was on the way to an appointment.

A lady who went with me asked me if seeing this place bothered me. I took a deep breath, and without a pause, I said, "Not anymore, especially not today." Although I was looking at the same parking lot, I saw, heard, and felt something different.

It's almost as if I pasted a picture over another picture. Instead of the memory of evil in that guy's eyes in the parking lot, I could now see a new empowering scene.

Instead of the guy loading groceries in the parking lot and the manager being nonchalant (as I was protecting my siblings and getting help), I saw something else: a new character.

It was a chance to reframe this moment and other moments where I have faced extreme evil in my life. Although I had already forgiven the man (and others), I still needed something. I didn't need to face them physically (even though I just hope they have changed their lives and are helping instead of hurting people today). In fact, until that day I didn't know what I needed.

For years I chose to feel like a victim from and in this situation and others, and as a result, I lived with a lot of fear. After processing more, I realized the human hero I had been looking for all this time was and still is me.

For years I chose to feel like a victim ... and as a result, I lived with a lot of fear.

From this realization, I have taken other situations in my life and looked at them in a different light. Celebrating what I knew at the time of those negative events, I have now been able to give myself compassion and see ways I creatively lived through those experiences.

Many times, I re-pictured them by seeing myself as a hero instead of a victim. I even wrote out a timeline of my life using information from diaries and intentionally resaw every negative situation from a better perspective, focusing on the good that came out of it and the lessons I learned.

I also realized in my life that a moment is just a moment. For a moment to be remembered or a future similar moment to be "triggering" (causing such emotions as fear, anger, isolation, fight, flight, freeze, etc.), strong emotions have to be added. Without emotional fuel, a moment in the past loses power over us and we can move forward from the parked, negative areas or memories in our lives.

So today, choose to see your life differently and resee your story. You are the hero in your story, too. A hero isn't perfect and doesn't always get everything right. Sometimes a hero even has to apologize or be accountable for their actions. Further, a hero doesn't always feel brave, but a hero always moves forward to overcome in the end.

Your life isn't over yet. It's time to do the work to get above the bad memories of your past that have you parked and unable to move forward. It's time to flip the script in your life's movie and reframe it. It's time to fly.

Riding Lesson #5

Realize you did the best you could with what you knew at the time of trauma in your life. Process and reframe those moments from your past by seeing them from a different perspective and flipping the script with you as a hero because you are still here. You survived.

Feel It to Heal It

It might hurt you to your core,
Might make you sweat through your pores.

It might mean sleepless nights,
It might mean you have to face everything that wasn't right.

It might mean you have to relive the situation in the dark
It might mean you have to face the menace of that evil bark.

It might mean pictures or occasions have to be reseen,
It might mean situations have to be redeemed.

It might mean you have to go back to your childhood,
It might mean you have to see where you once stood.

It might mean you have to release the emotions of a moment,
It might mean you have to let go of
overwhelming disappointment.

However, sometimes to heal it,
You have to feel it.

Oh, yes, sometimes to heal it,
You have to be willing to feel it.

All of it.

Joy on the Journey: Laughter Heals

On an airplane flight home from a vacation in Florida, I laughed so hard I was crying. I finally had to ask the lady beside me to save the rest of her jokes for when we got to the home airport.

While the flight attendants were going over the seat belt rules, I was attempting to not crack up due to the comments around me. As I tried to keep my composure, a military veteran said, "Listen to this; it's my favorite part." I tried to listen with a straight face as the flight attendant said, "In case of an emergency, make sure *before* you put your OXYGEN MASK on *to take off* your FACE MASK (during COVID). Otherwise, you will not be able to breathe." The veteran quipped, "Good point."

Then the lady beside me talked about her flying experiences and having sinus infections and asking a flight attendant for help.

She said, "Guess what she brought?"

I said, "I have no clue. Fill me in."

"Two styrofoam cups."

I was thinking, *Dear Lord, no.*

She went on, "Yes, and I put them over both ears."

What?

Then another traveler had a story about Montana. This caused a lady passenger to sing, "Where the deer and the antelope play." The guy's story was interesting until he mentioned three antelope walking out of a bar and a mountain in Wyoming whose name for so many reasons I can't repeat.

Finally, I just looked out the plane window, laughing as tears rolled down my face. It just kept going. Our whole section was a mess in a good way, and it trickled out into everyone else.

On the flight home, I realized the power laughter has to heal, strengthen, uplift, and break down barriers between people. I also remembered my Grandmother Scott, who encouraged me and gave me the freedom to laugh with her so many times about so many things.

> *I realized the power laughter has to heal, strengthen, uplift, and break down barriers between people.*

Finally, on this trip, I realized what a special gift laughter is on the journey of life. Although in all probability, none of us passengers on that particular flight will ever meet again, I doubt any of us will forget the fun we had together and how much we laughed.

If you haven't added laughter and fun to your journey, I highly recommend it. It might be watching a comedian or getting together with friends for fun. Whatever it is, I hope you find big and small moments to smile.

Riding (or should I say *Flight*) Lesson #6

Add things to your life that bring joy and make you smile, heal, and feel strong. It will make the journey more fun, and it's contagious!

Unlikely Friends: Free to Fly

People comment all the time on how amazing it is that we are so close. What is strange is how unlikely our friendship was at first.

I don't remember officially meeting her on Memorial Day, 2015. I wasn't in a good place. At her wedding to my brother, I was not included in the wedding party.

Inwardly I was a little bitter because of how close my brother and I had always been. I put on a nice face and said kind things anyway.

Time passed, and my relationship with my sister-in-law, Bethany, became more strained. Around that time, I heard a talk about the importance of forgiveness, getting over stuff, and truly letting go of resentment held toward others.

I had a long list of people to contact or let go inside. I remember calling Bethany soon after. I had already decided that regardless of whether she forgave me or not, I was going to tell her I was sorry for holding it against her all this time and at least ask. I also decided that regardless of how anyone reacted, I was going to let go of all the bitterness inside and not expect them to do anything.

I will never forget when she returned my call.

I was at the library studying during my last year of college. It was humbling to tell her, but she was kind and apologized for unintentionally hurting me.

It was crazy because unknown to me at the time, she was going through her own pain.

We cried together, and what I thought would drive us further apart actually brought us closer together. Today, I consider her a real sister and loyal friend.

Am I perfect at letting stuff go today? No.

I'm still asking for forgiveness and daily letting go of inward hurt toward others as quickly as I can even just inside. It's wild though—the freedom that comes as I allow others to be human as well as allowing myself to be imperfectly human.

> *I'm still asking for forgiveness and daily letting go of inward hurt toward others as quickly as I can ...*

However, not all stories end like this. Sometimes we have to set boundaries, especially if there is abuse involved or it's not possible to talk to the person for whatever reason. In those cases, letting it go internally or writing a forgiveness letter to rip up and toss helps to get rid of the bad emotions and hurt. I have done both.

With that being said, I'm grateful that forgiveness opened the door for Bethany to be involved in my life. Forgiveness has opened my heart to many others who have become the most unlikely, genuine, real, and true friends I know.

In 2021, my brother and sister-in-law gave birth to a baby girl whose middle name is Grace. That made me cry at the possibilities that forgiveness can open up in our lives when we get rid of bitterness.

I'm thankful for Bethany showing me through our relationship that imperfect (even in me) is sometimes just perfect. I'm also grateful she allowed me to share our story transparently with you.

Bethany shares her perspective:

I don't even remember meeting Grace. To anyone who has met her recently, I know that is absolutely crazy. However, at the time, I was dating her brother, and meeting his siblings was new and overwhelming for me. Especially sisters. I am one of three kids. I have two brothers. I had no idea how sister dynamics worked.

I have two brothers. I had no idea how sister dynamics worked.

I had my whirlwind romance with her brother, and I have only a vague memory of Grace coming in and out of the house a couple times, not really making eye contact with anyone. She had moved out and was in school, I was told.

Joseph (her brother, now my husband) mentioned her in stories from growing up, and I eventually figured out that she was the next sibling down in age and his closest sister.

Fast forward to our wedding.

My husband is a highly social person. He has like eighty good friends. He wanted all of them to be in the wedding party. Lol.

In our era, having different numbers of bridesmaids and groomsmen was not a thing I'd ever heard of. He wanted ten. I don't have that many close friends.

My number was eight. That's how many girls I could think of that I wanted to be in my wedding. So I pulled in girls who were closest to my age whom I felt at the time better acquainted with.

The wedding happened, and I rolled into married life, which was a crash course—moving states away, torn from everything I'd ever known and all the places I fit in, and plopped forty-five minutes away even from the people I knew in Indiana, to try and figure out how to keep house and be a wife.

I can laugh about it now, but there really was no honeymoon period.

We were immediately over our heads in unmet expectations and each other's various baggage, and I felt more alone than I'd ever felt in my life.

I felt more alone than I'd ever felt in my life.

We got pregnant, moved, and Joseph changed jobs—all the same year we got married. I do NOT recommend this combo to anyone, ever.

We found help and began to untangle our struggles, one piece at a time, but those first two years were difficult, to say the least.

Then one day I got a phone call from Grace.

She was calling to apologize for holding it against me that I had not asked her to be in our wedding and to let me know she was no longer holding it against me.

First of all, I was devastated and felt sick, and it was one of the biggest "facepalms" (faux pas) of my life.

I was grieved that I had done something so thoughtless, and I apologized to her from the bottom of my heart. A barrier broke that day, one that I hadn't even known was there, and I began to get to know Grace, one family gathering at a time.

Then she called me out of the blue one day when I was at home alone.

She had no idea what we had been going through, and I decided to let her in, a little.

Eventually, she was calling me from time to time, probably once a month or so, and I began to realize that I had found a sister I could be real with who wouldn't judge me.

Little did I know what a gift I received by gaining Grace as a sister by marriage. Sis has my back like no friend I've ever known before, and I've got hers.

I have truly never met a kinder or more gracious person in my life. She really does embody her name. And I never would have really known her if it weren't for the power of forgiveness.

Riding Lesson #7

Forgive yourself and anyone you are holding anything against. It's time to feel free and light again.

It's Beautiful To Be Alive

It's a beautiful thing to be alive,
To breathe in each breath.

It's a beautiful thing to be alive,
Have another day to start fresh.

It's a beautiful thing to be alive,
To dream and accomplish something new.

It's a beautiful thing to be alive,
To have friends who are amazing and kind.

It's a beautiful thing to be alive,
And live out the design placed on the inside.

It's a beautiful thing to be alive,
To forgive everyone and be forgiven.

It's a beautiful thing to be alive,
With the past too far behind to catch back up.

It's a beautiful thing to be alive,
To try something new, to share love in the world.

It's a beautiful thing to be alive,
With endless possibilities.

It's a beautiful thing to be alive,
To see the sunset and a new sunrise.

Today is new,
It's a beautiful thing to be alive.

Buried Alive: People Along the Way

This story always spoke to my heart when I was younger. In some ways I feel connected to it. In 2008, I entered it in a National History Contest and won first place, which included among other things a cash prize. Years later looking back over it, I see a new lesson. Happy reading!

On a ship, a young U.S. Navy sailor lies suffering. The year is 1918. Constantly in pain, he struggles to breathe, as his body becomes increasingly weak. Littered around on board are many crew members already dead, while others like him await their inevitable end.

Moment by moment, life fades from disease-ridden sailors. At length his body also slumps in a lifeless heap. Time passes, and the ship docks in a port in South America. Here supplies are purchased while the dead are removed to freshly dug burial ditches. Then the ship moves on once again out to sea.

Back in Indiana, Minerva slowly sits down on a wooden chair. Stunned, this young teacher's mind races to grasp the entire meaning of what has just transpired. Her childhood sweetheart, Ralph, is dead. Like so many others, his candle has been put out by the rapidly spreading flu pandemic. Tears stream down her face as she tries to pick up the shattered pieces of her life.

Knowing this is what Ralph would have wished, she at last consents, and they become good friends.

Months glide by in a haze. Slowly with comfort from Ralph's best friend, Carl, she learns to live without Ralph. Then one day Carl asks Minerva if she would date him. Knowing this is what Ralph would have wished, she at last consents, and they become good friends.

Meanwhile news circulates worldwide of increasing numbers of victims dying from the same influenza that Ralph contracted. Panic-stricken people begin wearing masks to avoid getting the flu. Meeting places in some cities are shut down, and meetings are forbidden.

Despite these precautions, unending grief rolls in like a monstrous river as the pandemic continues to wipe out thousands. However, there is little time to single out these fatalities, for countless other dedicated youth are also dying daily for freedom in World War I. While doctors carefully tend to wounded and flu-infected servicemen, specialists meticulously search in vain for a cure for the influenza that is killing more than the war itself.

Then suddenly, in 1919, the flu disappears. Warily, city meetings reopen and eventually citizens are no longer required to wear masks when riding the city bus. Although the influenza has ended, it has left its unforgiving mark. Around the world, fifty million lives, including half a million from the United States, are gone forever, wiped out by this humanly incurable plague.

Five years pass. At her grandparents' home, my Great-grandmother Minerva awaits a special moment. It is her wedding day, September 6, 1924.

Slowly she walks toward the end of the procession. The rich aroma of fresh flowers fills the air. Nearing the end, she approaches Carl, who is standing beside a good friend.

Moving closer, she stops next to the man she is about to marry. It is Ralph! Miraculously, he has returned, but how did this happen?

In South America, in 1918, a beautiful woman hurries on her way to the market. Coming around a bend she is startled as a low moan escapes from one of the burial ditches. She stops in shock! Slowly approaching the body, she turns and runs home to get her husband's help. Together the native family returns and takes the body home. For several months, they gently nurse the sailor back to life, unknown to anyone.

Slowly approaching the body, she turns and runs home to get her husband's help.

Then in health, the sailor, Ralph, travels to American soil. Here he is met by Minerva Jane, who has broken off her relationship with their understanding friend, Carl. At last married, Ralph and Minerva spend many happy years together.

Working hard, they raise eight children during the Great Depression. These children give Ralph and Minerva many grandchildren, including one who grows up to be my father, William Atherton. Then, nearing the end of their simple lives, with family around them, Ralph and Minerva occasionally reflect on days gone by.

Pondering on their lives together, they are inevitably drawn back. Back to the extraordinary time when Ralph was a young sailor and was rescued from being buried alive, when he was deathly ill, during the influenza pandemic of 1918.

This story was told to me by a relative before she passed. Today it reminds me of the importance of having good people and environments around you.

Riding Lesson #8

Surround yourself with uplifting people who help you feel alive. Your environment can mean the difference between getting out of the grave of your past or being buried in it.

It's the people along the way...

It was my voice teacher, Lola,
who encouraged me to write lyrics,
Who helped me hit notes.
She helped me gain confidence in knowing how to sing a song.

It was the people who fearlessly told their stories
Of overcoming and going on to be successful,
And gave me so many keys to change the way I thought.

It was the man at the gun shop who looked me in the eye
And said, "No, no, you are not the gun type of girl."
He never knew it for sure,
but he saved my life from suicide that night.

It was the man at the gas station,
The day my career downtown was finished
and I drove and got lost,
Who not only jotted down directions on paper
but told me to keep the faith.

It was the random lady I met in a parking lot
who gave me a bowl of rice.
Little did she know I didn't have enough money
for anything else other than bills that night.
Then she talked to me about life and things that helped her.

It was the officer who stopped me that night,
When I was swerving, tears flowing down my face
and I didn't want to go on,
Who told me his story and how he made it through.

It's the people along the way.

It was my Aunt Kathy who let me stay over at her house,
After long hours of work to finish college papers,
Who made me the best meals and then we talked.

It was my grandmother who let me live with her
when I worked in the city,
Who gave me a place to heal and laugh,
Who taught me the importance of humor,
especially through the hard times.

It was a life coach, Eli,
who helped me learn about patterns
And worked to help me make changes in my life,
Who has continued to teach me skills and be a great friend.

It was the countless medical professionals who encouraged me,
Even after my second wreck,
to keep a good mindset,
And helped me get my health back.

It was the ladies (including Kate)
who have been amazing roommates,
Who taught me about good friends,
It was the conversations that continue to make me feel good.

It was and is the friends and family members
(too numerous to list)
Who light up my life,
The ones you least expect but who are there.

It's the people along the way.

Who has been along the way in your life to help you
or encourage you to dream?
Who has walked a mile or two with you?
Who has helped you get this far
or encouraged you to reach new heights
you could never reach alone?

It's the people ...

Who are the people in your life,
and in whose life can you be that person?

Gratitude: What Matters

Dear Antoinette,

We met in an unusual way. That day I was dealing badly with rejection and depression, and I went for a drive to get away from everything. I looked everywhere to try to find a sanctuary. I felt like if I could find someone to talk to, I would feel better. Outside one building, I took a picture of a bus that had my name, Grace, graffitied on it, but no one was inside. I finally resorted to looking online for crisis line numbers. No one picked up. Finally, I drove away into the country alone in my car and cried. All I could think was, I need help! Suddenly, my phone rang. Someone was calling me back. It was you. You weren't going to call me back because you didn't know the number, but you heard my message and, although a little annoyed, felt pulled to return my call. When I answered, you told me a lot of stuff I didn't want to hear, so I was going to hang up, when suddenly it all made sense. Although neither of us wanted to talk to one another originally, that day we were connected, and the rest is history. Antoinette, you invited me into your family. You loved me unconditionally and let me call you at all hours of the day and night. You helped me learn how to break depression and rejection. You taught me to understand so much about myself that I didn't know. You encouraged me to forgive people, to be kind, and see what was truly behind things. You celebrated me and what I was doing. You were one of the first ones I called when I was struggling or needed support. You were one of my first friends. You walked with me through hell and back. I had built up walls so I wouldn't be hurt ever again, and you taught me

I love you not just for all the things you have done for me but for who you are.

how to pull them down. If you had not been brought into my life, I doubt if I would have loved people and even known how to reach out to others again. You are more than an inspiration. I owe so much of who I am to you. I love you not just for all the things you have done for me but for who you are.

I wrote this letter to Antoinette the day her son called and told me it didn't look good. Somehow, I could feel it was her last day on earth and she didn't have much time left, and so I wrote. Then I texted it to her son, and he read it to her. Shortly after that, she passed away.

Weeks later, he added my social media acknowledgment to her obituary, along with those written by her other kids. It read:

Antoinette was one of the most beautiful people I have ever met. Although she was beautiful on the outside, her soul was even more beautiful. We met in the most unusual way, as she lives states away. She loved me unconditionally when I was going through so much stuff years ago. She told me her entire story and helped me understand mine. She celebrated me and things I was doing. She was one of my first new friends back then as my life was being rebuilt. She was more than an inspiration! I introduced many of my friends to her, and she accepted them and loved them. I loved not only all the things she was and did for me, but I loved who she was. Her laugh, her wisdom, her heart. She inspired me to want to be so much more. Some people you meet and feel like they are too good for this world, like they were made for another one. That was her. Saturday, she slipped into eternity. Life is so short, and the price of love is painful some days, but I would not trade that price for having known her!

Today as I write this, I am thinking about how grateful I am that I had the opportunity to tell Antoinette what I thought about her before she passed. As my grandmother always said, "Don't give me roses after I am dead; give them to me before." She is another person I'm grateful for, and I'm glad I said everything I needed to along with giving her green-tipped red roses the Christmas before she passed.

As you read this, maybe you're thinking of those you miss. Maybe even a loved one who has departed. But today I want you to think also about those people you still have. In what ways can you show gratitude to those who have poured into your life or who need encouragement? What about through voice messages, acts of kindness, verbally, through letters, through cooking, fixing a vehicle, or some other way?

Tomorrow is not promised for any of us.

Riding Lesson #9

Life is short. Say the positive things you think and be grateful for the people and things in your life today.

If ...

If you only had one more day,
What is it you wish you would say,
What types of things would you do,
How would you want others to describe you?

If you only had one day left,
Who would you thank,
What apology would you say,
Who would you talk to instead of ignoring?

If you only had one day to your name,
What would you have to gain,
What things wouldn't matter anymore,
What worries would you leave at the door?

If tomorrow was your last,
What would you make sure was done fast,
What would be the most important things,
What would be the last song you sing?

My Ride or Die: Search for the Answer

I'll never forget leaving the hospital exam room and the therapist, trying once again to find answers to help me get through all the dirt in my life. I wasn't okay. That day I knew this wouldn't help me either. I could tell the medical provider cared, but it wasn't something she could fix. I also knew that the therapist and the counselor she recommended might be alright, but I needed something more.

(Disclaimer: I have been to all of these specialists at different times, and they have been helpful. I also would recommend them if that is what you need, as it may be the key to your personal breakthrough. I am just sharing here what was helpful for me with my unique situation, circumstances, and personality.)

At this time, I needed someone who knew how I felt, had been through something similar, and could help me heal it. Looking back today to my suicide attempt after that hospital visit, I see I was desperate. If I didn't get help, I knew I wouldn't make it.

I had already been searching, and in my mind, I would continue to search—if I lived that long. My search took me on a journey to study various religions and philosophers. This included driving to temples, lodges, and various religious places of worship.

(Note: I still have a deep respect for and am friends with people from all types of backgrounds. I feel it's a sign of maturity in life to be open to hear views, stories, and outcomes that are different from our own. In fact, I wish right now that I could hear your story and unique views. Everyone having different opinions is a sign we all have a brain.)

After driving and visiting so many places, I found it hard to know what to trust. Past hurt from (cult)ures (we all grow up and live in unique ones) in my past and the "dos and don'ts" seemed to bring up pain. Besides visiting places for answers, I tried to talk to people. Most couldn't understand what I had been through and couldn't relate. Some even said, "Get over it" and "You should be fine now." Or they called me unstable and unintentionally hit every one of my weak spots or trigger points before I learned how to heal from those so I could avoid reacting. At that time, I was trying to find peace, answers, relief from the pain, and a sense of belonging—what we all want in life if we are honest.

After driving and visiting so many places, I found it hard to know what to trust.

After the night I cried out in my car, "God, if you still have a plan and purpose, you have to stop me because I can't stop myself," I started to see a little light. The light started when I was verbally stopped in my tracks by the man at the gun shop. After surviving that, I knew I had been carried when I couldn't carry myself. I could feel it. However, the pain inside was far from being over.

Although years before, I had given my life to God after understanding more fully what His death on the cross had done to free me from the grief, abuse, pain, and mistakes of my past, I was still struggling. Even though through baptism, symbolically my past was spiritually dead and I felt a little more alive, I still had questions. I was on a search for truth and a way to get rid of the pain, depression, unprocessed trauma, repeated thoughts of events that made no sense, and suicidal thoughts.

Around that time, I made a deal with God: If I can't believe everything in the Bible, and if everything is not true for today, I'll chuck it.

After that, I started reading the Bible for myself without wearing lenses from my past, especially what religion had taught me about it. I found out much of what I had learned in the past wasn't true and God wasn't what people had made Him out to be.

Art also helped me in some ways to process what I was learning. Here is a painting I did during that time:

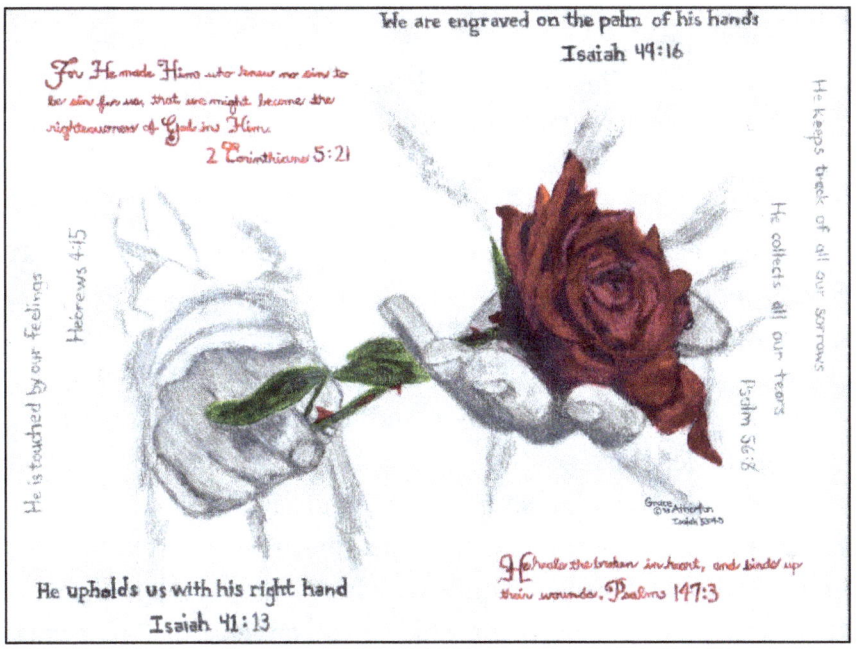

It is titled "Jesus Wants the Rose." The rose represents me and maybe you. The single raindrop over the thumb represents the tears; the torn petal represents the brokenness; and the nail print represents the unconditional love on the cross. I did it to represent how—just like during my suicide attempt—we all face or will face tough times, but Jesus is touched by our feelings. He understands our failures and mistakes. He keeps all of our tears, and He cares! He is there through any and all pain and mistakes. He wants us, even when we don't feel it, deserve it, or care! He holds us and carries us through situations we think we can't bear.

Around this painting I added verses I found in the Bible. One stood out when I looked at these words: "He heals the brokenhearted, and binds up their wounds" (Psalm 147:3 NKJV).

It was the best thing I had found to describe what had happened to me inside and outside when I was emotionally broken and at the time described how I was healing inside day by day. Just like a physical wound, it was taking time to heal, but through rest, care, time, personal development lessons (especially based on principles from the Bible), and the right resources, I started to ride above the dirt in my life.

As I read the Bible during that time, one particular story stood out. It was about a lady who was crying. She too was troubled by the demons of her past.

Around her, people didn't understand. Maybe they thought she was unstable. Her past was colorful. Her former life included prostitution and what some in the church circles of the day considered to be dirty work. The Bible doesn't give away all of her story. It doesn't say what wounds led her to that point. It just says that while she was broken, she broke open some expensive perfume and used it along with her tears to wash Jesus' feet and dry them with her hair. Culturally, people's feet were dirty at that time from walking barefoot or in sandals, so it was common, just as it is in some areas around the world, to clean people's feet when they came into the house.

People in the room continued to judge her. Didn't Jesus know who she was, her story, her mistakes, her past? He did. Yet, He still let her get close to Him and touch Him. Apparently, He was all right with her and her past. In fact, the more I read the Bible for myself, the more I realized that He looked more at people's hearts than perfection. He looked more at the heart than rules. He looked more at my heart than where I found myself the day of my suicide attempt or my past before that of sexual abuse, abandonment, rejection, and brokenness that led me there.

He knew that woman's heart, He knew my heart, and He knows your heart. He's unconcerned about imperfections or mistakes and can take the burden of them off of hearts. Everyone in the Bible made mistakes, little ones and even big ones. The only perfect person was and is Jesus. Our imperfections, mistakes, and hurts from our past are only signs we need Him. We need Him to heal us inside.

Riding Lesson #10
Never stop searching for THE ANSWER to your unique problems. Healing can take time, but it is so worth it.

Sometimes She Broke Boxes

She never fit inside their mold,
The way it had always been was old,
And sometimes it hurt deep to the core,
As she left behind the pain from where she was torn.

And sometimes she broke boxes.

Sometimes her story went around the world,
And sometimes her story stayed at a single door,
And still other times she heard the voices around,
Speak to her to move away from the peace she found.

In the One who believed in her now,
The One who decided her story could change somehow,
That her past would not define her future,
And her scars could be turned into something beautiful.

And sometimes she broke boxes.

At her lowest, she found her highest,
At her weakest, she found her greatest strength,
At her darkest, she found the brightest light,
In her brokenness, she found her healing.

And sometimes she broke boxes.

The tears could never stop her,
Her most expensive possessions
Paled in comparison to what she had found,
And so she traded it all out.

And through this process, sometimes she broke boxes.

The man-made structures
And useless traditions,
The protocol, the confinement,
The should-haves and would-have-beens,

No longer did she have to act
Completely to fit in,
No longer did she have to be passionless,
About the new things placed within.

And so sometimes she broke boxes.

Who is she, this woman stuck in time?
It's a story about a lady in history, along with a story about me
and maybe, just maybe
it's a story about you redefined.

About the times we break boxes.

Died for Dirt: Love's Everything

If you find yourself at this chapter, perhaps it's because you are curious, or you realize you can't do it all on your own in life. Like me, maybe you have come to the end of your own path. Maybe you're tired of religion and rules. Maybe, like me, you can't get out of the dirt, the cycles, and the mess, and you can't be perfect in your own life to earn your salvation (as hard as you've tried).

What follows is a simple prayer. Basically, it's about giving up the reins of your life and realizing you want Someone higher to help you on your ride of life. I prayed a similar prayer. In fact, I have prayed a lot of prayers (just talking to God) for God to go through the trials with me and be there in every moment, good and bad. Maybe you feel you need that too.

You might feel like me— that you have done too much wrong to be forgiven by God. Believe me, you haven't. In fact, He died for us while we were already sinners. Some of us still have to pay for things down here in the world, but with Jesus on our side, we can rise through His power above the circumstances even while we walk through them. Besides being saved from our sins and mistakes, we are promised a home in heaven with God and Jesus when we get to the end of this ride called life.

For God so loved the world that He gave His only begotten Son,
that whoever believes in Him should not perish
but have everlasting life.
(John 3:16 NKJV)

I will never forget realizing this fact for the first time. I was already loved enough before I was born, sinned, or hit planet earth for Jesus to die for and cover my mistakes, and so are you.

Then I read this in my Bible:

That if you confess with your mouth the Lord Jesus
and believe in your heart that God has raised Him from the dead,
you will be saved.
(Romans 10:9 NKJV)

I just needed to speak out the name of Jesus and believe in my heart that He died and was raised from the dead. So that's what I did. Below is a prayer similar to the one I prayed. If you are ready to give the reins of your life over to Jesus, you can pray the prayer too. The exact words are not what saves you, but believing in Jesus, what He did, and trusting Him in your heart is what does.

Prayer
God I am a sinner,
I need you to help me get above the dirt in my life.
I acknowledge I can't ride this out on my own.
Please forgive me for my sins.
I believe Jesus died on the cross for my sins
and rose from the dead on the third day.
Come into my heart and life and take the reins.
I need your help to get through everything I'm facing.
Lead me every day to the end of my life's road. Amen!

If you said that prayer and believe it, know that He is with you. Later, you might look back throughout your life and see His hand through everything. How do I know? Because I have experienced seeing His hand throughout my life, through the people He sent, circumstances He rearranged, and the peace He gave me. In fact, every chapter of this book is the story of His hand holding the reins of my life even before I knew it.

If you said that prayer and believe it, know that He is with you.

It doesn't mean more dirt or stuff hasn't or won't come. In fact, following God can sometimes bring more. However, it does mean that after giving Jesus our lives, you and I won't ride this life on our own without God. It means you can get His peace that raises you above the dirt even as you pass through it. It also means you can belong in God's family and be accepted and loved by Him.

And even if you do not feel this is for you, I hope we can both agree that Love is the solution to every problem in our world.

Riding Lesson #11
Take a chance on faith. Believe Love is the greatest thing in the world and the solution to every problem.

My Dad Likes to Play in the Mud

I used to think something was wrong with me.
When I was young, I made mud cakes with beautiful flowers,
Roads and sandcastles,
Tunnels and bridges dug in the dirt by hand,
I used to run through it and grow plants in it,
Throw corn cob stalks with muddy roots,
In friendly turf wars,
I created and made dirty things.
Sometimes, secretly, I still like to go mudding.

I think playing in the dirt was inherited.
You see, I liked to play in the dirt and my Dad likes playing in the
dirt too.
He makes clay people pots.
It's on a pottery wheel but if it's not quite right,
He breaks and reforms it.
It's messy, it's dirty, but Dad's near.
He's near the break and the remake,
So near.

In the break, it's never meant to stay that way,
It's never meant to be dirt clumps in a thousand pieces,
It's never meant to be dumped and left on the floor,
It's meant to be made into something new,
Each individual piece of brokenness made into a beautiful pot,
Through the reshaping and the fire,
It's dirty, but that's what my Dad does is play in the mud.

Something changed as I got older.
I went through a lot of dirt.

Have you ever had mud thrown on your name?
Your character ditched or times when you lacked character
when you were ditched?
Have you ever felt so broken that there was no way
to glue the pieces back together?
No strength to pick the pieces off the floor?
Maybe trauma from an experience?
Depression?
Brokenness?
Everyone leaving you on the side of the road in the dirt
during your darkest times?
Childhood or adult wounds so deep they hurt?
People letting you down or most importantly
letting yourself down?
Have you ever felt so low you hit dirt?

Well, the good news is Dad makes stuff out of mud,
molding, remolding, making stuff out of the brokenness
and the nothing.
Since the beginning he has been playing in the dirt,
When he played in the dirt the first time he made the first man.
It was dirty.

In fact, one of my Dad's sons became the dirtiest,
nothing, so he could experience everything we go through,
and cover all the dirt.
I guess playing in dirt runs in the family.

In fact, when everyone else looks down on others,
my brother looks up on his knees.
Just like he did with a sister caught cheating,
he writes stuff in the mud.

A new story.
The stones of accusation and shame get dropped,
Because he makes stuff out of mud.

Another time he mixed spit and dirt
To help a brother see again.

I know my brother got playing in dirt from Dad
because one time another son got his inheritance early
and spent all the money.
He went to dirty places and did dirty things.
He was all covered in pig pen mud.
When he finally came back home my Dad made him a meal
and covered his dirty clothes with a beautiful coat.

Another time Dad went after a lost sheep on the farm,
the one that got away, just like some of his kids do
from time to time.
It was dirty.
He went after it just like he does us and found it.

I am thankful my Dad likes to play in the mud!
Because with mud in His hands, He can remake anything.

Scars to Stars: Imprinted for Purpose

Only having one day left to live—sounds like a crazy thought, until it's not. It is hard to put that into perspective until you face something you never planned on.

That was June 1, 2022, for me. Originally, I never planned to share this. However, a week later on a plane from Texas, a lady asked about my bandage and after hearing about it, she said, "You have to share your story. All of it."

That day I was driving to see family. Although I had trouble with my phone charging the day before, it charged fine when I took it to the store to get it checked out. This day was different. As I drove, I jiggled the cord, trying to get it to charge, but it didn't help. It would not charge. Finally, I glanced down and tried to push the circular charger in farther and jiggle the wire more. Still no charge.

When I looked up, there was no time to brake.

Instinctively, I put my arm up just in time for impact. I had little time to take that in, as I saw the electric pole break and begin to fall. Quickly, I jumped from the car, leaving the cord and phone hanging out the open door.

Recently, at my job, I had seen a presentation on electric lines. The presenters spoke about jumping with both feet together and continuing to hop if you were ever next to live electricity to reduce the possibility of being electrocuted. It came back to me in an instant. I hopped and hopped out in a field as I noticed blood on my arm. I could hardly feel anything due to adrenaline. It felt like an out-of-body experience. Finally exhausted, I sat down and looked back.

I could hardly feel anything due to adrenaline. It felt like an out-of-body experience.

The pole and wires were down. Some of the wires had even started a fire in the grass. Then I noticed a car was driving toward the wreck. I waved and screamed for them to stop, and they did. Running around the wires, they came to me. From the other direction, a farmer ran toward my car. I screamed for him to stop. He did once he realized I was the only passenger in the car and that there were live electric lines down.

Finally, first responders arrived. In the ambulance, they looked over my arm and other bruises. I tried to make up jokes to keep myself from crying. Those around helped. Suddenly the workers mentioned that my arm had the Nissan Maxima insignia from the car steering wheel imprinted in blood when it flew out. I mentioned that in a week I would be an extra in a television series and wondered how I would cover the wound. (I eventually used a bandage that fit the time period.) The responders joked that I should instead do an ad for Nissan Maxima with the insignia.

When the electric company finally came, they turned the electricity off. I will never forget utility workers and the officers walking toward me shaking their heads. I had not seen my car up close and had no clue what to expect. I couldn't even remember if I had turned my car off. (I had not.)

By this time, one of my friends who was close by arrived and heard it as well. I still do not remember who said it, but it seems to ring in my head even now. "Ma'am, we are sorry, but your car has been completely totaled. It was completely hot (with electricity), and we just want you to know that we don't come to scenes like this where anyone makes it out alive."

For two days, I had flashbacks of the pole and how the impact felt. Finally, I got a different perspective (by reframing it), and the flashbacks left. It felt unreal at times. Then my arm, bruises, and swelling would remind me it was real, along with all the calls I had to make to square everything away, including insurance.

"We don't come to scenes like this where anyone makes it out alive."

Surprisingly, because I focused so much on what I was grateful for during the beginning of the healing process, the effects didn't fully sink in at the time. After coming back from being on a film out of state—a trip that included an emergency airplane landing—I was able to remove the bandages on my arm. The first day after having the wraps off, when I was finally by myself, I cried. I am visual and love things being special, moments being beautiful, and things being taken care of to the best of my ability. I thought about how I might have the scar forever.

That night, I cried for the second time since the accident. The first time was when the woman I met on the airplane told me I should share my story. That night, I just talked to God about how I was really feeling. How I knew His hand was on me the entire week of the accident. I told Him I was okay with wearing the scar, even though I wasn't very happy about it. One thing I asked Him was to please give me a different perspective of it, because all I could see (although it had a cool shape and my favorite car insignia) was the biggest physical scar I had ever had on my body.

The next day, a gentleman who has a radio program came up to me. The first thing he said was, "You know what your scar looks like?" I said, "Yes, a Nissan Maxima insignia." He said, "No, I was thinking something else. It looks like lips—a kiss from heaven." It didn't hit me then, but when I got back to the cabin I was staying in and looked down at my arm, I smiled. Later on, another person said, "You have a nice battle scar." Again, I smiled, because I realized that my scar was a reminder. A reminder of where I had been, what I had been through, and a symbol that God shows up in the middle of our imperfect humanness, in the middle of a wild situation, and can give us a beautiful perspective.

As I wrote about this, I decided to do something hard for me. Hard because I love beautiful things. I love having things look nice and not be broken. I am sharing something that I am learning doesn't have to make me feel self-conscious or "less than." Thanks to the woman named Andrea on the plane, who encouraged me, I am sharing this story as a reminder that we all have scars—whether others can see them (like mine or maybe yours which may be more extreme than mine) or not (like the invisible scars we all carry). However, when we take them to God, who wears scars as well, He can turn them into beautiful reminders that He was with us even through the fire where we got the scar(s)!

So back to the thought of having only a day to live. I have thought about it a lot since that day. How would I live? How do I wish I had lived? How would I treat people if I knew today was it? What would

I prioritize that I have not so far? What has to change in me? And finally, what do I have to trust God with that I have no control over? Maybe this will make you think about questions like that also.

Life, even a long life, is really short. However, now when I look down at my arm (whether the entire scar stays or goes), I can smile as I did the night of the accident, when I was grateful for one more chance at life. Smile at the imprinted reminder to make each day and moment as imperfectly beautiful as possible while keeping what matters most in mind!

Riding Lesson #12

Take time to think about your scars (emotional, physical, mental) and the areas in which you've been imprinted with lessons and purpose. Using your unique talents, take a small step to use what you have gone through to encourage or help someone else to get through their pain.

What's in Your Hand?

What's in your hand?
It could be someone's provision.

What's in your hand?
It could lead a nation to freedom.

What's in your hand?
It could protect the weak.

What's in your hand?
It could pay off debts.

What's in your hand?
It could be the next invention.

What's in your hand?
It could feed those suffering in hunger.

What's in your hand?
It could bandage the broken.

What's in your hand?
It could change the mindset of humans.

It's easy to see the deficit, instead of the plus,
It's easy to wish we had more
instead of starting with what we've got.

So starting today …
Use the gifts in your hand!

What's in your hand?

It could be "a pen mightier than the sword,"
It could be a painting that catches the world's galore.

It could be a picture worth a thousand words,
Or it could be music that changes
where a nation's headed toward.

It could be a dance to catch a scene or a sign,
It could be your treasure, your talent
or anything that will go on throughout time.

What's in your hand?

Chapter 13

Bulletproof Dream: Stars Shine

Loading my gun, I faced the target and unloaded every last bullet. Bullseye, bullseye, bullseye.

As a special ops agent, I suddenly realized my worst fear. Behind me I could feel the pressure from what seemed like a warzone of the enemy coming after me. I could feel the words, the stalking, the questioning, the trial, the past. The only problem was, I was supposed to be at home safe, with active duty years behind me. But now, my gun magazine was empty. I scrambled to find even one bullet. Finally, I found one, but it took several attempts to fit it into the opening. I held a flashlight and the gun in the direction where I could feel the presence of the invisible opponents, trying to see and take in who they were and how they had found me.

At that moment, flashes of past traumas seemed to be coming back to me as I tried to keep myself steady. With gun pointed and flashlight to the rafters, I looked. Suddenly I could see them—the enemy. No, there was only one. Lit up by my flashlight, I stared into the eyes of a child pointing a gun at me. For an instant, my heart stopped beating, and my breathing became heavy. Then I realized it was ONLY a plastic toy gun. Slowly, we stared eye to eye. Gun to gun. Face to face. Something in this kid felt familiar, similar, even alike. Suddenly, I realized I was staring at myself as a child. This was not an enemy. Letting out a deep sigh of relief, I startled myself awake. I was dreaming. I was not and had never been in the military, special ops, or on a battlefield. I could have pinched myself. However, in the early hours of that morning, I realized something etched forever on my memory from this dream that felt lifelike: *I was created to be elite in my specialty, gifts, and purpose. There was only one thing chasing me: my destiny and who I was born to be, reflected in who I was as the child in my dream.*

Just like the dream, I hope today you live the design of who you were made to be before you hit planet earth (especially if your childhood was rough). I hope you become who you were made to be as if you had never gone through any trauma and dirt.

> **I hope you become who you were made to be as if you had never gone through any trauma and dirt.**

I hope that person stands up. I hope when you look destiny in the eye, you see a grown version of your greatness, and I hope you shine. I hope you become elite in your field, in your gifts, and I hope you realize that there is only one thing chasing you that matters. Your destiny. Your greatness. Who you were born to be.

So aim for that target. Aim for that vision. And shine with your life, with the spark given to you before birth, until you rise above the dirt—mentally, physically, emotionally, and spiritually.

You, the horse, and I all have something in common. We were born for greatness. We were born to fly!

Riding Lesson #13

Don't dim your shine and who you were made to be. Focus more on your destiny than your past and your fears.

When Did the Star Stop Shining?

When did the star stop shining?
What kind of dark evening was it?
What clouds covered the light?
What made the night feel unright?

When did the star stop singing?
What drowned out the voice's feeling?
When did it think the sound was rough?
When did the miles make it feel not enough?

When did the star stop directing,
What kind of lie did the wise stop accepting,
Since once many stars were used by a crew,
To bring freedom "through its drinking gourd"
followed by a few.

When did the star stop timing,
The days, the years, the seasons changing,
What kept it from keeping things on track?
Can we ever get it back?

When did the stars stop telling,
Something deeper beyond Zodiac and astronomy,
Serpens-snake, Virgo-virgin, and cross—
When did it stop—the story of redemption coming from loss?

When will the star start shining?
When will the clouds roll back in the evening?
When will all things feel right,
When will the voice have a new song taking flight?

When will freedom ring from above?
When will the season change to love?
When will refreshing water lead north?
When will there be more humans rebirthed?

When will the Star(s) start shining?
How about today,
How about tomorrow, how about forever!

Each one of us lives in a world,
Sometimes it can be dark but under the clouds
there can still be light in the soul,
So ...

Let it shine,
Breaking through the dark,
Let it sing,
Breaking through the silence,
Let it direct,
Breaking through to freedom,
Let it time,
Breaking through the standstill,
Let it tell,
Breaking through the lies.

When did the star stop shining?
When did the star stop singing?
When did the star stop directing?
When did the star stop timing?
When did the star stop telling?

How about not today,
Not tomorrow, not ever!

Stars aren't meant to hide,
They and you are meant to shine!

Riding Lessons

#1: Commit to investing time in yourself, especially to learn. You are priceless whether you feel like it or not!

#2: Purpose is inside you. Do not wait for the perfect time or conditions. Grow and bloom on and in the mess.

#3: Accept yourself fully without comparison. Then work on the thoughts, emotions, and words you are feeding your mind and mouth about yourself and your life.

#4: Dream again. Write, draw, picture, record what you would do if you had all the money, time, and energy in the world.

#5: Realize you did the best you could with what you knew at the time of trauma in your life. Process and reframe those moments from your past by seeing them from a different perspective and flipping the script with you as a hero because you are still here. You survived.

#6: Add things to your life that bring joy and make you smile, heal, and feel strong. It will make the journey more fun, and it's contagious!

#7: Forgive yourself and anyone you are holding anything against. It's time to feel free and light again.

#8: Surround yourself with uplifting people who help you feel alive. Your environment can mean the difference between getting out of the grave of your past or being buried in it.

#9: Life is short. Say the positive things you think and be grateful for the people and things in your life today.

#10: Never stop searching for THE ANSWER to your unique problems. Healing can take time, but it is so worth it.

#11: Take a chance on faith. Believe Love is the greatest thing in the world and the solution to every problem.

#12: Take time to think about your scars (emotional, physical, mental) and the areas in which you've been imprinted with lessons and purpose. Using your unique talents, take a small step to use what you have gone through to encourage or help someone else to get through their pain.

#13: Don't dim your shine and who you were made to be. Focus more on your destiny than your past and your fears.

About Grace Atherton:
I Know What It's Like

I know what it's like to be different,
To grow up in a sub(cult)ure and feel misunderstood.

I know what it's like to be called fat, and to starve my body,
To deal with low self-esteem, comparison,
and to be told I was less than.

I know what it's like to be passed over,
To be told my personality was terrible.

I know what it's like to be almost abducted,
To be abused mentally, physically, emotionally, sexually,
and deal with trauma.

I know what it's like to want to sing, write, paint, and speak,
To fail many times at each and deal with debilitating fear.

I know what it's like to deal with rejection,
To be talked about behind my back and excluded.

I know what it's like to have my brother almost die
from appendicitis,
To find true friends, including my grandmother,
and lose them and her to death.

I know what it's like to have my heart broken,
To feel like no one is pulling for me.

I know what it's like to be called out,
feel speechless and shaken to my core,
To be told I am going crazy, am unstable, and am not capable.

I know what it's like to wonder where I would sleep,
What I would eat.

I know what it's like to go through job loss,
Transitions, moving around, and multiple car wrecks.

I know what it's like to face medical challenges,
To be sick for long periods of time with no solutions.

I know what it's like to deal so badly
with depression and panic attacks
That I actually attempted suicide and wrongly believed
the world would be better without me.

I know what it's like to hear negative comments
by those who assume untrue things about me,
Based on how I look and act now.

I know what it's like to be ashamed of my story,
To hope no one would ever find out,
so I could pretend nothing happened.

I know what all those things and many more are like.

I know what it's like to hit dirt ...
And to hope no one ever reads about some of that dirt,
especially in a book like this.

However, it was those dirty moments that made me realize that kindness is beautiful, that words matter, and that hurting hearts should be handled with care. Now when I hear someone "labeled," I typically want to get to know them and see who they truly are that others may have missed due to a past mistake, misunderstanding, or just plain dirt. Because countless people did this for me, encouraged me along the way, and gave me steps to move forward and upward, I am no longer defined by those words or experiences.

In this book, I have included the lessons I learned in a simple format so you too can not only experience a little from my life's ride but also see your ride in a different way and fast track the beginning of your rise above the dirt in your life to reach your unique destination.

For free content to encourage you on your ride of life or to contact me with your feedback or questions, visit: www.graceatherton.com.

References

Chapter 1
Lesson 1 - Psalm 139:14

Chapter 2
Lesson 2 - Job 14:7-9, Isaiah 61:4

Chapter 3
Lesson 3 - 2 Corinthians 10:12, Proverbs 18:21, 3 John 2, Psalm 103:5
Poem: "A New Start" - Psalm 126:5-6

Chapter 4
Lesson 4 - Proverbs 29:18

Chapter 5
Lesson 5 - Psalm 147:3, Luke 10:30-37, 2 Corinthians 10:5

Chapter 6
Lesson 6 - Proverbs 17:22, Nehemiah 8:10, Proverbs 15:15

Chapter 7
Lesson 7 - Matthew 18:21-35, Matthew 6:12-15, Ephesians 4:32

Chapter 8
Lesson 8 - Proverbs 13:20, Proverbs 22:24, 1 Corinthians 5:1-11

Chapter 9
Lesson 9 - 1 Thessalonians 5:18

Chapter 10

Lesson 10 - Proverbs 25:2

Poem: "Sometimes She Broke Boxes" - Matthew 26:6-13, Luke 7:36-50, Mark 14: 3-9

Chapter 11

Lesson 11 - 1 Corinthians 13, Romans 8: 35-39

Poem: "My Dad Likes to Play in the Mud" - Jeremiah 18:4, Isaiah 45:9, 2 Corinthians 5:21, John 8:1-11, John 9:1-7, Luke 15:11-31, Luke 15:1-7

Chapter 12

Lesson 12 - John 20:24-29

Poem: "What's in Your Hand?" - Exodus 4:2, 11 Kings 4:1-7, 1 Samuel 17:26-50, Matthew 25:35-40

Chapter 13

Lesson 13 - Isaiah 60:1, Matthew 5:15-16

Poem: "When Did the Star Stop Shining?" - Matthew 2:1-12, Genesis 1:14-16

www.ingramcontent.com/pod-product-compliance
Lightning Source LLC
Chambersburg PA
CBHW071335130626
46556CB00004B/1918